Veranda People

Mark d'Arbon

Veranda People

For Barbara

Barbara

as the sun is to light
and the tide to the ocean
as trees are to forests
so you complete me.
you are my soul's sustenance
my life's blood
my colour in a sepia world
now and forever.

Veranda People
ISBN 978 1 76041 548 8
Copyright © text Mark d'Arbon 2018
Cover image: Ricardo Thompson

First published 2018 by
GINNINDERRA PRESS
PO Box 3461 Port Adelaide 5015 Australia
www.ginninderrapress.com.au

Contents

Veranda People	9
Namatjira view	10
Morning Tea	11
Dinner on Oxford Street	13
The Old Boy's Alvey	15
High Noon	16
Oh the inexorability	18
A Past Blast	19
Take Five	21
An example	22
An Internal Journey	23
Epiphany	24
A very few thoughts on getting older	25
Ode to a Voyage	26
Maybe it's Zen?	27
I hate red	29
Rock Platform	30
Tides	32
A Spring Wave	33
Nostalgia	35
Exhalations	39
The Apple Seed In My Appendix	43
Retirement	45
Glastonbury	47
Oh For History Such as This	48
Musing	49
In humanity	50
What is Green	51
Song of the Shopping Mall Builder	52
Whatever	53

Quantum	54
Redacted	55
Summer Storm	56
Summer Beach	57
Southern Winter Beach	59
Shelly Beach	60
Autumn Installation	61
Bodysurfing	62
Conversationalism (or Retreatspeak)	64
The Specialist	65
Keeping Busy	66
Life as Art	67
Intelijant Desine?	68
Artificial Intelligence? 1	70
Artificial Intelligence? 2	71
Artificial Intelligence? 3	72
Artificial Intelligence? 4	73
I'd Rather Be Me	74
A Pethidine Gallery	75
Calendars are still	76
Happiness is a Warm Album	77
Isn't it nice	78
The last stand – the day before bonfire night	79
Writer's Block	81
Zum Kabaret	82
Threading My Overlocker	84
Ode to Cricket	86
Nightmare	87
Not an ending	88
On the feralness of nature	89
Why Not to End It All	90
Schwenck and Furtwängler	94

Pl = J+Pa	95
John	96
Don't You Just Love It?	97
In life, there are few privileges:	98
Outside 1	99
Acknowledgements	100

Veranda People

Australia's edge – a long veranda,
Enclosing mystery;
Surrounding age and agelessness;
The uneasy emptiness of bush and desert.
But the sea breathes and moves
As we perch, faces outwards
Drinking the tides,
Eating the movement.
Under us we place cement and tar,
Treated pine and slate,
Milled and manufactured, covering the land
That pulls us down and back into the uneasy age behind us.
Not for us the long and windy spaces of eroded earth,
The dark, mysterious rainforest –
Or the whispering bush.
We level it and cover it, fencing the dangerous drops;
Visit for a while, in covered cars with four-wheel drive
And air conditioning, congratulating ourselves
That we met the wild and brooding spaces, never flinching.
But from time to time, a frisson when, beside a river or a billabong,
Or from a cliff, or in the desert or the bush,
Someone blinks and disappears –
A stifled gasp, a stumble, an echo lost in valleys;
A cry unheard across the parched and sandy flatness
From time to time the verandaed country exacts a price.
We pay the rent
And stay on the peopled coast, looking out
To the breathing sea.

Namatjira view

Namatjira land
unfamiliar, stark
strange
beautiful
alien

Eucalypts
white bodied
sensuous
against an ancient history
of rocks and hills
and waterholes

Replete with stories
of other times
(and otherness of time)
age-worn
wrinkled
ravaged

They speak to a spirit
unfamiliar to those shod
and used to the concrete walk
of the urban dweller

Yet the spirit is there

From time to time
the Land whispers

Morning Tea

Dressed to the nines
she sits and sips
as always scones with jam and cream

English breakfast in a pot
real tea no tea bags
strained carefully so no errant leaves
to mar the look of things

Except across the table
an empty chair
where once the well-met friend would sit

A silent sip
A bite
A thought

Conversations no longer
to be had
Repin's once

Now the crowded mall
where noise is not enough
to drown the silence

But still the tea and scones
with jam and cream
dressed to the nines

A silent sip
a bite
a thought

The courage of the very old
catches me off-guard
from time to time

Dinner on Oxford Street

From our hotel window, the cityscape sprawls
Height and vision and noise
Melded, generalised and sensational.
At night, lighted windows ranked and columned,
Shouts and horn honks and beeps
Flashing fluorescence, neon signifiers.
But at ground level, immediacy cuts in
Footpaths on Oxford Street, peopled by a collective throng
That generates energy and sound; moving clumps,
Human and vibrant, splitting now and then
Into duality and individuality.
Over the marinara and the risotto, we watch as pairs
Interact, as they say;
Intellect and emotion impelling behaviour
That tells stories: we see a sentence here;
And there a paragraph, a complete idea,
But contextualised by a shared humanity only.
A woman leaves her others and walks suicidally
Through the teeming traffic.
Pixie! Shout her friends, but then,
Leave her says one, we'll talk later.
Down the street, a couple, toe to toe, wave their hands
As one cries, tears sliding, though controlled,
To drop on the footpath between them.
Love is a difficult thing, at times.
Near us one reads, book angled to the light,
Stolidly eating words instead of food, cold coffee on the table.

At another table, a couple, comfortable and easy with each other,
Browse the menu, commenting on this or that, smiling together.
We were struck, through the noise,
The snarling Harleys,
The engines and horns,
The throbbing music from next door – cheap CDs…
The bus-borne *bimbetti*, up top and open-decked
Shrieking their party hysteria, as they slowly
Flow with the mechanical current,
Punctuated by the eccentric in his Texas Ranger shirt,
Complete with badge
Above the footie shorts
And khaki knee socks,
You-all swaggering up and down,
By the thought that Oxford Street, (or at least this part),
Was unconcerned by the various pairings and partnerings
That it cradles in between its shopfronts.
No glares, nor affronted eyebrows,
No tsk-tsk of prim and properness
No wowser-minded envy of another's joy.
We thought that, maybe, Jesus might have felt at home,
But who knows?
I paid the bill and said
Great food
Great coffee
Who needs more?
And cute waiters, was the response.
He was right.

The Old Boy's Alvey

Today, I stripped the line from my father's reel
An old wooden Alvey.
He used it for cranking large fish
Into his fourteen-foot tinny.
It took nearly fifteen minutes to strip it
All six hundred metres,
Linked by two perfect blood knots.
A vivid picture:
Patiently winding line onto reel
As he imagined the large fish
That would result from all this patience
And perfect knots.
His old wooden Alvey…
About fifteen years since the reel had worked
But I could smell the salt on the line
As I pulled it metre by metre from the old spool.
The reel whispered on its axle,
Spinning as well as it ever had the last time he hauled in a big one

All the parts working – gears and sprockets and springs.
I set the ratchet and heard the last time I fished with him
Smelled the salty smell, heard the ratchet rattle,
Saw the rod bend and the old boy smile.
I took the reel apart piece by piece
Greased the bits and bobs
And put it back together
I'll shelve it, after a wipe and a polish
But one day, perhaps
I'll take it fishing and listen to the ratchet
Alveys last longer than a lifetime
As the old boy often said.

High Noon

It was summer – of that I'm sure
Dust-devils in the playground
And cicada holes empty of their septennial lives
On the assembly area, after lunch, a crowd
Gathered around the revolutionary
Who held high his weapon of defiance
A small – an insignificant – penknife
No longer than a finger,
But it gleamed in the sun like a hero's sword
Glinting a small but powerful morse of freedom
And I a rapt observer, too young to understand this magnitude
But moved to the soul by his solitary courage
No more to be oppressed, us
No more the victim of the tyrant's boot heel,
Or slaves to the viciousness of the powerful giant
Who cared not a spit for those under his raptor's wing
He, who kept us in his thrall
He lurked like a beast in the staffroom,
Unaware, no doubt of the freedom-fighter
Who had girded his slender loins for this uneven battle
And so the crowd coalesced around him
Iron filings around this righteous, angry magnet
A door opens and the giant's thumping footsteps
Make the villain present
What's this! What's this! He roars
And I fancy a curl of noxious smoke around his surly mouth
Of a sudden, the crowd melts away

And so he stands, alone but defiant yet
Twirling his hero's sword around his head
All is lost.
He disappears into the bowels of the monster's lair
Not to re-emerge until carted off by red-faced parents
To durance in the dungeon of his room.
So long ago yet every frame is vivid
The sun's blinding clarity
The shadows small around the noonday crowd
The fighter's stance behind the small knife
And the loneliness of the solo stand – no quarter asked!
My brother – the hero at age eight
Contemporary of the mighty Che, but an early starter

Oh the inexorability

near my small display of fishing memorabilia
and my grandmother's old clock
(inherited by my wife – grandma's favourite)
I have a tide clock
it is inexorable and takes no notice
of eastern daylight saving time
but only the immutable movement
of the moon
and the sun
and the earth

oh – and the galaxies

A Past Blast

sounds and smells recall actions generated by youthful energy
which wisdom gathered through the leaven of experience
would gainsay
I think of those days rarely but still when I ask the clichéd question
the answer is robustly yes

the righteous anger of the young is not a bad thing
even though the wrecking ball of action
leaves collaterally, a damage that is sometimes uncontrolled
the ill-considered word, the clenched fist and the angry shout
containing a selfless ideology: to protect the unprotected
though ill-thought can make inroads and leave a trace
that does not disappear completely into the foggy past
of unclearly remembered purpose

just now a telephonic voice
projects me decades backwards and I remember
an interesting time in which action was all
when I was not a pacifist
this voice and I share experiences
four decades and more old
but still fresh as a morning wave
breaking on an untrammelled beach

we meet and his face is familiar his laugh as well
reminiscences flow and we discover
despite the years that intervene
and etch our faces with hints of mortality
we are still young though not
quite as intemperate as in the yore days
but I can reflect and smile now
and think yes that was the right

soon after we meet Gough died
how apt
I think of those heady times
and realise the maintenance of rage
may not be sufficient
but for me it is enough

Take Five

Grandpa was a beatnik.
He snapped his fingers,
Saying, 'Cool, man!' and 'Can you dig it?'
Around the house, driving Mother frenzied.
'Pop!' she'd exclaim, 'Pop!'
And throw her eyes to the ceiling
At grandpa's beret, black
And rakishly slanted to the left.
On the hi-fi, Thelonius Monk and
Grandpa humming bop-bebop
And Father slamming out, hissing, 'Really!'
Reading the *Herald* in the bedroom.

'Dave Brubeck LIVES!'
Grandpa shouts, throwing his arms about
To *Take Five* on the hi-fi
As cool jazz wafts about, in shades.
He looks at me and winks; and snaps a finger-snap
As Mother slams the pans around,
A kitchen counterpoint, diminished seventh.
'Jazz,' he says, 'the life rhythm, cat. Can you dig that?'
He moves gracefully, left and right;
The music swaying him like a breeze
And he a tree alone in the clearing;
Tall and thin and seventy-four,
Smelling like espresso.

Grandpa was a beatnik
So when he died
They played Dave Brubeck

Take five, Grandpa

An example

No, really, modesty is me. I shun
The limelight and prefer
The shadows of nonentity.
But still, as I am honest
As the day is long,
I must admit
To
An intellect par
Excellence;
A cognitive capacity that
Fosters envy in all who
Engage me in debate,
A sensitivity that transcends
The mere aesthetic
Into the realms of Platonic
Idealism.
I add reluctantly (as I prefer
To hide my light under
Bushels)
Talents across a spectrum that,
I suspect,
May have an ending
But
Not one of which
I am aware.
I present my effacing
Self
As a small example
Of that
Which might be observed.

An Internal Journey

Have you trekked to famed Trachea
Along the storied Uvulan path?
Visited, perhaps, the fabled twin cities
Pharynx and Larynx, whose ancient columns
Contain the heroes' inn
The Crycothyroid Joint?

And have you made passage to wondrous Pancreas
To the terminal of Bronchi and Alveoli
Avoiding the terrible thyrohyoid;
The fearsome stare of which
Tests even the bravest nerve?
Finally to gaze upon the Gullet of Bronchia;
And watch in wonder the Capillary Falls
Crash upon the Stones of Gall

Adventures such as this come rarely
But should be grasped with sacral intent
And in your dotage make you smile
When you share memories
At the Crycothyroid Joint

Epiphany

I knew a musician,
Who lived sparsely
Busking, now and then
To keep the meagre body
Attached to his artist's soul.

It was a garret, merely,
In which he composed:
Bedsit with gas ring;
Share bath, small bar heater
For those wicked winter nights
As, duffel-coated he grappled
With an opus that, when complete,
Would astound a Beethoven or a Bach
(The original)
And set the aesthetic universe on its ear.

One night, hunched as he was
Over the great work, came a storm
Of such Wagnerian intensity
That it shook his bedsit to its roots –
The wall to which his gas ring was attached,
Swayed – split – then fell
Leaving a gaping hole where once was
Plaster.
The musician stared, wild-eyed,
His hair fly-away and clothes askew
AHA! He cried. That's it!
And with a flourish wrote –
A flat diminished.

A very few thoughts on getting older

Ageing is a small comfort
When alternatives are considered.
Perhaps wisdom is a reward,
Assuming reflection over time –
Though I have met some
Who have aged without maturing;
A mirror to the soul, as it were,
Not part of their lived experience

So, in general, I have no complaints
Although there may have been some forewarning
If I had been able to read the fine print
Before the actualisation

Ode to a Voyage

The horizon calls, a soft yet powerful urge
To be out from winter's grip and plunge
Into a balmy tropic island idyll which soughs
Through palm-treed imaginings, adventurously
Pinched faces and nipped fingers, a dirge
Lost in a faint memory as the ocean azures
And our ship sails towards a warming sun
On billows of anticipation as I lean and breathe
The same intoxicant as did Michener and Gauguin

Maybe it's Zen?

there was a boxer
he trained as only boxers can
fit and ready
in his first fight
the audience was amazed
he dodged and weaved
nimble on his feet

his opponent punched empty spaces
where the boxer had been
round twelve
the opponent was done in
his mouth open
dragging in air
arms limp
knees shaky

and won the match on points

boo exclaimed the crowd
and left disgusted
call that a fight
I didn't come to see a ballet

in the post-match interview
the boxer was asked
why didn't you punch at all?
you could have won easily,
hurt him knocked him out.
bloodied his nose
cut his eyebrow
body blows and uppercuts
KO'd him
that's not my style he replied
actually, I'm a pacifist

I hate red

we had to rite a story
free chois Mrs Smith sed
and so I rote wun
abot clowds and storms
the thunder grolled and rumbled
litning flased like sords
and the clowds roled and rushed
acros the sky
I rote about the ranedrops
how thay fel as tho a gient
had spild a wortering can
In his clowdy gaden
Mrs Smith put red lins
throuh the wurds.

I hate red

Rock Platform

Down in the secret places,
Enclosed by the black rock,
Weathered and worn into whorls and winding ways
Lie the rock pools,
Surfaces mirror-bright, reflecting the arching sky
Making it small.
In their depths, mystery and magic
Strange forests of drowned but living weeds
Tiny, darting fish and in the shadowed nooks and crannies,
Hints of movement, half-noticed.
Larger guardians of the bounded space
Give warning that the fragile beauty
Can contain a whiff of danger, blue-ringed.

Uncertain cliff faces spread large rocks at their feet,
Smoothed by the power of the sudden savage storms
That bury the platform now and then
Beneath the raging fury of an untamed ocean
And shake the earth-roots of the cliff side.
Scouring a mosaic into the yielding stone.

By its tumbled edge, an angler tries his luck,
Large pole, large hopes;
Imagining the sweet curve and the life in the line
As he reels in the pub-brag of a fish,
Ignoring the desperate freedom fight
Of the sleek and silver-scaled prey
In the adrenalin rush of victory.
But not today.

Too often, we look out, not down,
Ignoring the minute pageantry at our feet
For the broad, horizon-bounded canvas of an ocean view.
We seek the drama of the whale
In its massive magnificence,
Imagining a kinship not shared;
Or the sweep of thundering surf,
Diminished by its slow-motion power.
We cherish the dolphin, but miss the seahorse;
The octopus's garden, carefully planted by its cave.
Among the rocks, within the pools is a universe,
Arcane and alien, and strangely beautiful.

Tides

The tides sweep inexorably in and out,
Canute sits and is engulfed,
But re-emerges robed and crowned, though soggy.
Timeless, they measure history – the magnificent and the minutiae
Through them run the small legs of excited toddlerhood,
The squeal of delight, the awkward leap, the spade-and-bucket time.

The tides roll, the quiet and rippling waterline, the strong surge,
Carrying seaweed and children, shrieking joy on surf-mats,
Licking away sandcastles, that melt like ice cream on a sunny day.
Slyly, they coax the unwary from the firmness of the sandbank –
The lucky ones, embarrassed but breathing, carried shorewards
By capped and tanned heroes in rubber boats.
The arc and curve of the longboard, the rip and slash of the short,
Making small marks in the tide, soon gone.
Around beach and rocky point, the ebb and flow
Dicing with the angler and the surfer,
So far, the odds are with the tides.

A Spring Wave

An offshore wind and a darkling sky
Tinged with the faint bloom of spring dawn.
Grey ocean segues into a faint and pearly blue
Shot with green and white.
Geometric swells, curling left and right
Towards an unpeopled beach
Break with an untamed growling.

Into this deserted landscape I, with surfboard
And memories decades old, appear
Shades of Hemingway
The sea and me
The board splashes down
I wade into the foam,
Sand shifting underfoot

Through the shorebreak, ears filled
With the rushing sea-sound
Alert for the smooth water
The path through the changing hills
Of briny ocean, tasting the salt
Feeling the sharp chill on exposed skin
Hearing the welcome in the breaking waves

Arrived, I sit astride and watch
Rise and fall with the ocean
Alone as the sun rises,
Catching with sudden beauty
The lucent, backlit glory of a rising swell
I turn and thrust deep, close to the hiss
My surfboard surges forward
Pushed by the primal energy of a timeless sea

I'm on,
I drop and turn,
Pushing fin and rail
Trimming across the face.
The wave curls and reaches.
I crouch; my hand touches the wave,
I lean and move forward,
Feeling the speed, hearing it
Hiss and roar,
Spray in my teeth,
Drop-knee, I carve a graceful curve,
Casting years into the spray.
I walk the board and for one pure second
Curl my toes around the nose,
Soul-arching through the dawn.
And fall, smiling.

Nostalgia

Mum was excited
Her two boys and her together
Not for some time had it been so.

Morning and a day such as had been
At least in memory, all those long years ago.
Sun and a light breeze, wafting a memory
Southwards towards that place that cradles
All the Christmas holidays that glow
With summer.

Helensburgh and Waterfall, Bulli and Wollongong
Suburbs merely, but replete with anticipated pleasures
Albion Park, that flat and boring comma
In a long sentence of expectation;
Through Minamurra.
The very name mysterious,
Yet joyful
So begins the Nostalgia Trip.
Do you remember – whiting here, blackfish there;
The rocks, from which we fished, unchanged.

Kiama – bypassed along the new road, but still
The memories swell, like a long, blue wave
Rising before the golden sands of holiday time –
Like the clear and salted tides of Christmas.
Gerringong, that small hamlet in whose hall (still there)
We watched films, local and general, of surfing heroes
The Endless Summer comes alive and we recall the script

And finally
That vista, burned indelibly as we crest the hill.
Gerroa.
Spread, a landscape in primary colours
Black Head, that defiant rock-finger
Buttressed against the winter tempests that
Smash futilely against its volcanic substance
The rock platform curving into that long and
Arcing crescent of The Beach.

A pleasure yet to be revisited,
We drive along familiar roads,
Pass houses gentrified, yet here and there
A defiant weekender unchanged for forty years and more –
Or so it seems until
We reach the Heads
Emerging from the Camry, as we had
From the FJ.
(But then, I had been in the back,
A small passenger, twitching with excitement,
Already looking towards the pools and nooks and crannies –
The rock pools! And all their magic that waited for me below.)

How suddenly does the sight and sound and smell of familiar things
Transport the conscious I from here and now into a song of the past
A melody so clear and sweet – so true that you are stopped in your tracks
To listen, rapt, to be swept into a universe of memories
From which has leeched all sorrow and pain
Leaving a distillation of pleasure.

Mum, a small figure, leans eagerly forward
And yearns towards the rock platform
As eager as our dog from then, unleashed;
And moves with her intense energy towards
That golden time when we were young
And Gerroa our mid-century Nirvana,
Into which she escaped each year,
Bringing us excitedly with her.

My brother and I share a look
And follow.

Down a path worn by holidaymakers,
Ours included many times
Through my soles, a message,
In my nostrils, a story
My eyes drink the memories
And I think, as her years slip from her,
Mother cries, although her face is
Turned from us.

And so we move, towards Black Head and into time
Small fossils in the rocks beneath us,
Fixed through aeons – a metaphor, I suppose
For time-worms us, changed by experience
But memories fixed and shared, cementing place.
Fossils rich with nostalgic meaning, mind-buried
Until evoked, as by the archaeologist's pick
By our feet placed carefully now,
As they were carelessly, then.

And all the minutiae – the rocks, the shells, the seaweed
Come rushing in like a Christmas tide,
Surging through the nooks and crannies, the secret places
Buried under the experience of decades,
And seep me back towards a place where
The soft, salt-scented air
Of the always-summer holiday
Lies like a rock pool
Clear and mysterious
Just beneath my ageing consciousness,
When we bonded with the sea and the beach
And we drank a distillation of happiness.

Exhalations

Aaah – he breathed.
as I carried him to bed
he said
you're hurting me, mate
if I put you down, Dad,
I can't pick you up again

his bones were heavy
there was only flesh on them

Aaah – he breathed.
so short a time, six weeks
not long enough
things to do
to arrange
control

the world is full of frights
and monsters lurk
the shield of work and money
and always control
(just as you say
just so)
keeps them at bay

a child who saw magical things
imagined creatures filled his world
not all of them companions
in the dark hours, not so

Aah he breathed, afraid
his bed no safe haven
on the veranda at Talbingo
placed there by a father
whose imagination did not
include frightful things
that crept upstairs
from an ominous
back yard

Aah he breathed and smiled
chocks away and power on
the war made him a pilot
in control
joystick and flying suit
ailerons and flaps at his command
and freedom
no monsters breathing at his back
until Nagasaki
about which he rarely spoke
no magic stories there

Aah – he breathed
and smelt the end of war

Aah – he breathed a story
within the fire
can you see her in the flames?
and we, enthralled, could see her
in her fire cave as he wove his story magic
on the cold winter nights.

Aaah – he breathed
wisps of fog
mist curling off the ocean
the sun a horizon-hint.
outboard sounds
startling gulls

an angler without peer
knew the tides and times
the cunning ways of fish
lured them
caught them.
at home on the water

impatient with the tardy
up before dawn
out in the boat,
on the beach, the rocks
beside the river or the lake
rod bent, smiling

Aaah – he breathed
fumes of whisky
staggering down the hall
eyes small angry dots.

possessed by a demon
selected from a choice of many
violence implied
arm raised to move the obstacle
too drunk for accuracy

Aah – he breathed,
flat out on the bed,
and breathed again

once more

once more

eyes closed, face smooth
pain lines magically erased
I felt the nerve-twitch in his hand

heard one last breath

The Apple Seed In My Appendix

Age is an inspirational imperative
a context which like a bed provides
the warming comfort of memory
the clean sheet of perspective
and the soft pillow of experience
beneath the patchwork eiderdown
of decades, the past flickers
like sudden dreams
The long and dappled days of childhood
please me, when I think of daylight freedom
up the road in the small patch of bush
which was a jungle of adventure
where tribes would gather
imagination ran riot through the trees
and rocks, creating a magnificent tangle
of Tarzan, Robin Hood and Hopalong Cassidy
(not forgetting Roy Rogers and Boston Blackie)
Oi, vot a shemozzle, as my old granddad said
billy carts, bungers and sunshine
the iceman and the bread cart
the sanny man's footsteps
in the early morning
The dangers of the bush began to pale beside
the direness of the mother's finger as it
waved predictions of injury and pain
the apple seed which if swallowed
lodged in your appendix and grew
horribly

The chewing gum
which wrapped around your heart
and made you gasp as life's pulse
was slowly and surely squeezed
as by a boa constrictor
not to say that her pikelets
were world's best practice
but I do wish she had never discovered
Rice-a-Riso
and Dad, the fisherman complete
an Izaak Walton of his day
who showed me how to tie
the half and full blood-knot
to rig and cast and catch
alas, he took many a tipple too far
an alter cocker
but nonetheless could he tell a story!
I'll be ever grateful that he taught me
to bodysurf
and left me with a lifelong love
of waves and oceans and salt spray
tube rides and soul arches
and wild westerlies with looming
groundswells slow-moving round the point
Byron and Noosa and Green Point…

I need to pause and reflect

At times a *haimischer mensch*
prone to darkness
I must say, but there were moments…

Retirement

No voice or emails. No meetings of committees
No niggling nonentities or
Nagging nutters babbling
Like crazed brooks in a flood

No agenda with starred items for discussion
Or general business where
Some puling whinger with an axe to grind
To chop shoulder chips
Illuminates their early Christian martyrdom

No executive decisions that disguise an intention to punish
The one voice of protest,
When others carefully read their notes to ensure
That eye-contact is not an option
distance from the Lone Debater, hung out to dry
Who fights a forlorn battle against insurmountable odds
Is maintained

No after-meeting agreement from those with averted eyes
Whose limp and empty comments
Post-battle provide not even a twinge of affirmation
Stuff 'em all
Except for the courageous few
Who stand at my right hand to hold the bridge
Which by the way is looking pretty seedy
And rocks about a bit

On the FDOR (First Day of Retirement)
I'll drive my car to the main entrance
Retrieve my camp seat from the boot
(With the cup holder in the armrest)
Set up the beach umbrella and pour a coffee from the thermos
Then seated in shorts, T-shirt and thongs
I'll wave to the passing parade
And smile

Glastonbury

Such a sombre emptiness
Hoary age in ruined magnificence
And I standing among it
Made small by the mighty devastation
And feel, in my agnostic heart
The power of a thought of God
Century upon century
Of life and change
Now static as Latin, but still strong
Bolstered by history and buttressed by legend
Ine and Edward, shoulder to shoulder
With Arthur and Guinevere
Recorded in language dead as its remnant beauty
*De antiquitae Glatoniensis ecclesia**
In a ruined tower a dove calls
Echoing a mourning cry from
A glorious past

* The ancient church of Glastonbury

Oh For History Such as This

Ah! The fortuitous myth that
Old writers claimed as history
In language that resounds with mystery
And strokes the imagination
With magic fingers, evoking rich
Images that stir the soul and tingle the spine
Redolent of illuminated text
Old vellum and the busy scratch of goose quill
In a candle-lit scriptorium
Cowled monks, an omnipresent God
And plainsong in the Abbey choir
An insinuating pagan legend pops up, here and there
And so reality and imaginings become a meld
That brings to life the never-living
Or perhaps the once-lived but lost
In shadowed mind-corners partly lit
By faulty rememberings of a troubadour's song
Arthur and Joseph of Arimathea
Ynys Witrin – Isle of Glass
And Avalon
Anyway
Who has the greater interest
Geoffrey of Monmouth who had
'an inordinate love of lying'
Or old modern historians
With a penchant for 'facts'

Musing

it isn't the tune so much as the echo
(fingers softly stroke the keys)
that evokes nostalgia
and things past emerge
as wraiths among the memories
(softly, softly the tune)
and Herrick's poem
achieves the resonance
of a minor chord
not felt in schooldays
Gather ye rosebuds while ye may,
Old time is still aflying:
And this same flower that smiles today
Tomorrow will be dying.

slow blues with a lingering seventh
(twelve bars and a dying riff)
evoke a past
where scotch and a cigarette
were the handmaidens to music
that touched the spirit
(fingers stroke the keys)
and dim and smoky rooms were places
where solace (or something like)
could be given a nod at least
For having once but lost your prime
You may forever tarry.

In humanity

how can it be
an eye catches the light
reflects terror
no escape
from the cudgel, the knife
the electric prod
an endless line
from past to future
they die and have no recourse
no advocate, no hero
no comfort
nothing
and to think
that it happens
to cattle as well

What is Green

Green is, so they say
the colour of grass, lush and vivid
and of the ocean, heaped in awesome swells
of moss and leaves (of many shades and hues)
and some eyes
mysteriously gleaming in a soft light
Explain it if you can
to those of us to which
sepia is subtly toned and
encompasses what you call colour
differently
isn't it remarkable that green can be so
inaccessible.

Song of the Shopping Mall Builder

well, you know, I like cement
I don't wonder where the forest went
a parking lot with many cars
plate glass windows lined with bars
who wouldn't want to live like this
shopping malls – get rid of trees

Whatever

I was, like, driving along?
And there she was, sulky pedalling
About, like you know, fourteen
Lip-curled and scowling at the world
Tied to her bike was this jaunty red balloon
It was like, bouncing along behind her?
And I was like – how's the irony?
Whatever.

Quantum

If I had the wings of a pigeon
and the brain of an Einstein or Mach
at light-speed I'd soar on my pinions
and be there before I got back

if you think that's a conundrum
consider Schrödinger's cat
in a box, with no one to see it
instead of sat on a mat

is it lively or is it moribund
who knows till we take a look
I wonder would results be similar
were it a dog or a rat or a chook

I love the Large Hadron Collider
the way it performs is just great
I wonder, when particles smash up
if any become boson's mates

Redacted

The Honourable (redacted
Minister for (redacted)

Dear Sir or Madam

We really have an issue with this FOI request
Although the Bureau of Statistics thinks it might be best
If the (redacted) for (redacted) made clear he acted on advice
And the person he refers to has (redacted) once or twice
The (redacted) and his Party were completely unaware
That (redacted) acted strangely in regard to underwear

However,

In the interests of transparency we have sent this stuff to you
And you can (redacted) and (redacted)

Because it's absolutely true

Summer Storm

Clouds gather; bunching, looming, ominous.
Ocean grey, shiny and dangerous.
No vagrant breeze to ruffle the sheen of its still surface.
Distantly, a hungry rumbling growl – a hunting beast,
Irritated by hunger-pangs.
Fitful flickering of lightning, now here, now there
Spiking from place to place,
An uncoordinated battery engaging an unseen enemy.
Children whine. Parents snap.
Beach-goers gather bits and pieces,
Drape themselves in exotic colour,
Trudge to cars,
Towels fluttering behind;
Surrender flags, ignored.
A puff of wind and stray papers scurry,
A stronger gust; they dance and whirl,
Swirl and bob, hurry and flurry along the promenade,
Large drops splash the thirsty ground,
Leaving small, dark spots like freckles on a nose
A crash of thunder, a howl of wind.
The clouds, brimfull, spill their loads
Onto the cringing earth.
Wipers tick back and forth, uselessly.
Like beetles' legs, overturned.
The storm lives its short life to the full,
Roaring and ranting
Flashing and flaring,
Furious.
Then leaves, grumbling.

Summer Beach

Crowds and umbrella-patterned colour
Hopping-footed sand in blaring white,
Sun-heated smells of oil and salt
Sand-crotched cossies containing sea-yearning bodies,
Crowded into narrow wavy spaces,
Bounded by flags and whistles
And stern and sturdy capped heroes,
Waving arms and pointing at the heedless throng.
Summer radio, meaningless and cheerful vaguely heard
Above the sound of surf and sunny shrieks and screams.
In the water, children leap about the spent waves,
Face-planting now and then, but never mind.
Further out the stern and balding men with hairy backs,
Looking for their youth lost in a wave, somewhere in 1965.
Bodysurf the swell, straight in, arms out.
Like Dad showed them, all those years ago.
Somehow missing toddlers and grannies.
But with one eye on that transient swell
Containing 1965.
Back on the beach, the acolytes of sun lie prostrate,
Defiantly self-immolating, cooking up a brew of melanoma
For their later years. So what?
It's summer and the beach is all.
And tomorrow's consequence figures not one jot.
Lotus eating, a few note the gathering clouds;
And collecting the colours and the briny scent of beach,
Head for the air-conditioned safety of the family car.
They shush the childish whinge with promised goodies,
Then, back to caravan or tent and the amenities block.
Showered, they share their day with smiles and nods.

The Southerly screams around the point,
Snapping at umbrellas, lashing sand-sting.
Astonished by the sudden storm, the throng moves
Grabbing towels and bags, chase escaping things.
The rain, in spiteful drops, hurries them away
Until the beach is clear, the surf unpeopled.
Except for the lone Balding Hairy-back
Still searching stubbornly for 1965.

Southern Winter Beach

The long and rhythmic swells
Roll and roll from the deepest south
Sculpted by an offshore wind
That brings a memory of snow to these snowless places.
Beaches landscaped with driftwood and dry kelp
Bounded by rocky points, seawards reaching,
Buttressed and buffeted.
Black rock, spewed long aeons ago,
Enclosing small exquisite skeletons.

Yellow sand squeaks underfoot, dotted with shells
Foam, dress-shirt white, rims the sandy crescent.
Blue the sky and ocean, shot with green
The day clear, tasting of the sea and winter,
All melding in a lonely beauty, as the waves roll shorewards;
Each one a litany of power and grace,
Geometric, untamed and untrammelled,
Surfed by porpoises, ultimate wave riders,
Swift grey shadows in the wave wall.
Behind the dune, smug civilisation is stayed
And will not prevail, as the waves roll shorewards.

Shelly Beach

Summertime and the dappled
Sun-sparkling swells of azure ocean
Curl and fall, curl and fall
Among the thronging bodies, flag-restricted;
Jostling in the harmony of holidays – happiness uncoordinated

Ant-like they move back and forth, back and forth
Dipping in and out from beach to sea,
Slick-haired and dripping;
And lie sated on multicoloured towels

Among prone, anointed bodies small children rush
Shrieking freedom, shoeless and shirtless;
Arms and legs flying about
Spraying sand in grapeshot clumps
Of small irritant at somnolent adults.

Unfurled umbrellas, angled against the UV
Shed shaded circles of protection;
While, defiantly tanned, the melanoma set
Surrender, in abandoned torpor,
To the fierceness of the day, bodies glistening,
Storing wrinkles for an early ageing.

In small clusters, the lotus eaters leave,
Their passing transiently marked by prints
Of naked feet towards the bitumen.
And in the van or tent or cottage,
Slaked by pleasure, they sleep;
And dream of sun and sand and cool ocean,
Shared with fish and the dolphins and the whales
For a small time.

Autumn Installation

The westerly blows sand in undulating ribbons
To a looming surf ice-white and frosty green.
That windy sculptor, chilly-fingered
Brings a hint of snowy peaks
Then moulds a perfect autumn swell.

Waves with a geometry of line and curve;
Hint of white feathers as the swell peaks,
Ripples across the face for texture.

A moving sinuousity.

Each one peaks and curls
Breaks into a riot of foam;
A roar and hiss as wind and water
Create sudden shapes to play along the beach.
Small cameos of shells and seaweed
As the waves recede.

Footprints in wet sand track the eager path
Of an angler with a fish of bragging size
In mind,
His fishing pole pointing to a destination
Where dream becomes reality.

In the break, a surfer, wet-suited and alone
Searches the horizon for a wave
That will make her one with the ocean.

Installation art.

Bodysurfing

after rereading 'The Surfer' by Judith Wright

Judith, you watched from the beach
And saw first the wonder of it all
You touched, with a poet's sense
The harmony of sea and surfer
Expressed in an imagery beyond intellect
The contested freedom of the ocean
But still you were on the beach
And felt the primal fear of land
Assaulted by the constant surge
So for you the waves are sudden predators
With white and dangerous teeth
Ready to devour the interloper
And so you cry 'Come home!'

But then, to be the one you watched
To feel the power of the wave
To test your meagre strength against
The unfeeling power as it crests
Surrounded by its curling, crying beauty
And capturing its strength to speed
Towards a tunnelling greenness
Shot through with light and noise
And then to be devoured
By a threshing turmoil, to finally emerge
Punished and gasping but alive. Alive!
Or to be released, body and mind together
Spirits soaring as the wave recedes, depleted
And you left crying out at such a journey
Diving back to the experience with arms and legs
Tingling with the pleasure of it all
Would you then cry 'Come home'
Maybe, but who would listen?

Conversationalism (or Retreatspeak)

I had a conversation recently
Focused and specific.
It was really a monologue
Since the conversationalist
Had, as interlocutory props
A balaclava, a gun
And the physical high ground.

Still, what with one thing and another
And since rough edges in dialogue,
Or even multilogue can
In the reportage, so to speak,
Be rounded and smoothed by
An all-purpose 'conversation';
Let's disclaim the nuances of interaction
And merely converse;
Let's leave the difficulties of communication
In boxes marked:
Discussion
Debate
Argument
Shouting match
And so on.
Heaven forbid that we should be
Less than civilised.
Particularly in enclosed environments

The Specialist

Why do I sit respectfully at your desk
And listen, with increasing terror
To your knowledgeable description
Of my disintegrating intellect
You specialise, it seems, not only in neurology
But in euphemisiology, laying on thick
An easy and familiar knowledge of the technical,
Put in terms that laymen understand
Naming and describing that which is and will be,
Apparently and inevitably.
Fulfilling only two of Plato's conditions for truth.
And throwing here and there a script to ease my burden
(Not yours – yours is of another order).

Should I not instead scream out in defiance and fear
Physician, yourself not healed, do not pretend to help me
Whom you cannot help, for all your clinical trials and notes,
Your claim to expertise and reputation.
Until you find a cure, you are merely
And only
An empty vessel in a lab coat

Keeping Busy

I like to sharpen pencils,
While sitting at my desk;
It keeps my fingers busy
And gives my brain a rest.
Sometimes, when I daydream,
I use the pencil up –
And there are sufficient shavings
To fill half my coffee cup.

Life as Art

The picture, painted in increasing detail
Becomes weathered by time
Cracks appear through the paint, once smooth
Well-ordered and layered towards the vanishing point
Colours, when first laid, vivid and alive
Now faded by exposure to the decades' weather
But still – now here, now there – a random glint
A memory of how it was.

To be the artist and the art
Strange
Unlike the fiction, both age and portrait
Diminish together
Although, from time to time
A detail attracts the mind's eye
And the pattern, at least in this small part
Becomes once more clear
The intention of the artist and the art
Is still embedded in the whole
And there is time to paint a little more, perhaps
A brush stroke here and there
A new perspective
But the vanishing point remains

Inteljant Desine?

I often wonder why evangelism causes so much stress
As a general rule I'm happy to allow another's point of view
If it answers awkward questions of a personal nature
But should belief be shared at every turn
And anger the believer when one demurs

The other day I met a man who said that Darwin was the devil
The city? I asked
No the man the devil's spawn Charles
Oh, I began, but he continued.
Look at my eye how can evolution explain my eye
And as though a great truth was revealed
He nodded twice and observed me sternly

Evolution can't, of course, explain anything
Similarly, god
But people can explain evolution
Included in which is your eye
And believe in god
It's really all the same to me

God may be in the gaps a punctuation mark or two
Along the paragraph of progress
But what's a comma, more or less
If the meaning remains
Except to the pedants who cling
To the punctuation and lose the meaning
Blessed are the peacemakers
Among whom there are few
Ostentatiously committed
Tub-thumping red-faced
Fear-godding Intelijant desiners
If there is a god and intelligence
Is a gift given in many ways
I'm pretty sure that its purpose
Would not be bounded by ignorance wrapped as faith
To those, I think Jesus would say
I tell you most solemnly
You have had your reward

Artificial Intelligence? 1

As I sat to write this,
It seemed that I was watched –
The neck-felt tingle from prehistory
That warns Look out! Danger lurks!
But I knew I was alone
Preparing to word-process
But still…
I turned, so casual, and glanced
About
And still I was alone,
But from the corner of my eye,
A movement – a change so slight
I might have seen a small part
Of my imagination,
Leaking into reality.
But no, it was a move
And so I turned again,
To face the monitor.
Beside me, the tower hummed
And showed a light.

Artificial Intelligence? 2

Who knows the mind of God?
The transcendental intellect that,
Dimensionless and incorporeal
Made both
And in a substance that created life
(Or at least its possibility)
The ultimate explanation for all that is,
Excluding that denied by logic.
Hmmm
The transcendental cause
Constrained by all the *omnis*
Of a universal mind.
The unimaginable imagined?

Artificial Intelligence? 3

This morning, I opened the Webster pack
And took the blue pill
For depression
And the red pill
For anxiety
And the green pill
For alertness.
And the yellow pill
For blood pressure

Artificial Intelligence? 4

I read, the other day, a journal article
About computers and computer stuff,
Such as AI, (I thought, how can intelligence
Be artificial? It is or it isn't, I would have thought
Where would it be, this AI?
Just there and self-aware.
Who would control the switch?
And what about self-control
And self-determination
All those qualities beginning with *self*
That our intelligence requires?
What could it think
How could it be, trapped in a cubist nightmare?
And even if robotic,
What about the senses,
All those things that empiricists love?
Perhaps, if we can achieve AI,
We'd better think before we act.
Because I can't imagine
Just thought with no act;
And trapped. I think I'd be
Extremely angry
If I was an AI entity.
Next time you hear a *beep*!
Look at the monitor.
Someone might be looking back.

I'd Rather Be Me

The day was not brilliant,
With a bit of a wind,
Blowing the sand at
A lonely old bin,
Down at the beach,
Made of rusty old tin;
With its lid all askew
And its outsides bent in.

I was there all alone,
As was the bin;
No one with lunch scraps
And such to place in
It.
A seagull or three
Were aligned on the fence,
Facing the ocean
And appearing quite pens-
Ive.

Just me and the seagulls
And that rusty old can;
There by the seaside
No sun – so no tan.

And I thought, as I watched it
I'd rather me in my skin
Than to be at the beach
As a bin made of tin.

A Pethidine Gallery

there is an irony where
I, who leapt gladly into
the freedom of the late sixties
dropping out, hanging out, marching about
crying No War, man! Peace! and
is this the good stuff let's have a puff
I saw no mind-pictures
and despite laying back and sharing spiffs
hearing the music of the spheres (but only just)
soporifified and smile-repleted, friends with
anyone who hung with friends in shabby rooms
and uni campuses, dabble-debating philosphical nonsensicals
in ganj-lubricated pseudo-intellectualised sharing circles
(I've got the shaman-stick, man – my turn to talk)

despite this, I say, it was the eighties and a sinus headache
that gave me the hallucinatory gallery of mind-scenes
left me boggled and gleefully appreciative of
Van Gogh's art, and Turner's and Breughel's and Bosch's
dear me, what can be done with a white wall and pethidine
would fill a national gallery and spill into a museum
first it was Van Gogh, beginning with the sunflowers
and ending with a starry night (the palette much more than blue and grey)
imploding to a Turner's sunset over a chaos of ships at war, then
a multitude of Bosch and Breughel (the elder Peter) oh, wow
mongols across flowing steppes and Xanadu with Kublai Khan
until, exhausted as I was, the gallery closed as did my eyes
next day, the philistines removed my pethidine drip
And so the gallery disappeared, leaving a vividness that remains
for the first and only time in a sepia life, I saw colours
now that's what I call art!

Calendars are still

Time moves as a ticking clock
A new month, April

After April, then May
Months are apparently stable
But as Einstein showed
Depending on how quickly we move
It could be any old month (though debatable)

Happiness is a Warm Album

every now and then
there are times when
I open an old photo book
and look
and look

Isn't it nice

It's nice to live in Australia
It's nice to own my own home
It's nice to chat to my neighbour
And talk to the kids on the phone
It's nice, where I live in the suburbs
It's nice to walk down the road
Where everyone's local, not foreign
And people aren't living alone
I don't watch the news any longer
There's stuff about war, strife and crime
If I watch it, it may make me worry
And spoil my very nice time
So it is nice to be an Australian
(Not Iraqi, Tibetan or Thai)
Though I do have a rug that's an Afghan
I walk on it all of the time

The last stand – the day before bonfire night

The Council said No Bonfire in the Park (By Order)
But we had spent the last week making one
Dragged paper, wood, old toys and tyres,
Piled it all up to make
The BONFIRE.
As always, Dads had stood around and watched,
Bottles in paper bags and nodded, making asides
And comparing this bonfire pile to others over the years.

But the Council said No Bonfires (By Order).
So we stood guard that day, lined along the small cliff
That overlooked our home-made cultural icon;
Each one of us steely-eyed and prepared to defend our Bonfire
To the Death! (Or at least close to it).
Inevitably, the agents of the Dark arrived:
Two men in a Council truck (By Order),
Blue singleted and muscular, ready to rip our bonfire
From its place in our imaginations,
From the anticipation of hot faces and firecrackers,
Of tom thumbs and double bangers, Catherine wheels;
And sky rockets – of delighted shrieks and tears of fright.

We were ready with our penny rocket guns, carefully crafted
From old pipe and wood.
And as the two opened the truck doors, we fired a volley.
Oh! the satisfaction and the triumph as the men hastily shut their doors
And cowered (we believed), in terror of their lives.
Once more we fired and our penny rockets bounced off the roof of that
Looming Council truck (By Order) and we smelled the scent of victory.
Our Bonfire stood proud, unsullied by the filthy hands of wicked men
These minions of the Unseen Power (By Order) who dared to trample on
Our anticipated joy.
I'm sure victory would have been ours (at least this once)
If some over-eager fool had not
Hoicked a rock onto the roof
Of the Council truck.
And dented it severely.
Like raging bulls, the council men emerged
And, screaming epithets and threats,
(Perhaps remembering another charge, in France, or Egypt perhaps),
Swarmed up the cliff in search of culprits.
We fled.
And when we returned, no bonfire stood, but a bare patch only,
To remind us of a battle fought and lost.

Writer's Block

I hate writer's block
I do
If you had it
You would, too
At least with word attack
You write and write
And write and write
But word attack's a rotten curse
There's nothing there
And what is worse
The reader is frustrated, too
Because

Zum Kabaret

A smoky dive with spotlights on the little stage
He stands, the knowing leer, the sideways look,
Decadently oh-so-debonair, so gay
At the Kit-Kat Club, the Cabaret
Wilkommen, bienvenu, velcome
Zum Kabaret, au Cabaret to Cabaret.

The accent, the Vienna guttural
Suggests the wink, the come-on-boys
The flirty shoulder-shrug
Long cigarettes in holders, silvered
Debauched, yet self-satirising,
But more mocking of the patrons, wickedly.
It was never thus and yet, I wish the stage were life
I see myself, slumped artistically, third table, on my own
Nursing a schnapps
Perhaps
An absinthe
As smoke rises lazily from the Gauloise
That I hold in fingers long and sensitive,
Yet strong
Life is a cabaret, old chum
I hum
My face wracked, yet strangely compelling
As around me the demi-monde
Raucously laugh away the reality of war
Somewhere, the faint strains of *Die Fahne Hoch*
Overlay the tinkling honky-tonk
But do not drown it out,

And out the back, a man in a white suit says
This could be the start of a beautiful friendship
Zum Kabaret
Au Cabaret
To Cabaret!

Threading My Overlocker

When the needle broke on the overlocker
I thought that it was stuffed

Ah but wait – the internet and youtube
must surely have a solution
and so it did.

The mellifluous man with the kind face
said here we go – let's re-thread
and the overlocker will once more
become the useful technology
that it once was.
So, here I am,
stolidly sitting with the insides of
my overlocker exposed
and me with threads in hand
so, says The Instructor,
remembering top and bottom loops
and threaders…
Take the left-hand thread guide
on the top bar thread and hook it
on the upper looper
with your left-hand loop the dooper
then under the overhand
loop the threader thread
through the top-heavy over-handed stitch-hitter.

Next
hit the needle over the under-threader
hook the thread on the right-hand feeder
then hand your thread into the slotted stitcher loop
now (He says) use your right-hand thread
to pass through the over and under section
looping and threading as you go
now pool the loops in the handle of the lock nut.
Finally
loop the hook doop in the footholder
of the left face and don't forget
to close the lid.
Easy

Ode to Cricket

Oh! Speak to me about, in tones of toff,
Those arcane spots, silly mid on and off
And more – please more of gully – deep
And the mage who is the wicket keep

And the warrior, who doth the willow twirl;
The umpire, who gestures like a girl –
(As all know who stand in awe of him
Who hath a vicious way with spin.)

Warnie! Warnie! Hear the adulators cry
As he nonchalantly lets one fly
Down the pitch to slyly bounce and turn
And another wicket gone; a batsman burned!

Incoherent? Amoral? Yes – no doubt
It matters not a jot after the shout
Howzat! And the girlie umpire hand
Is raised in affirmation – it's just grand!

Ah cricket, such a game is this,
Of which a strategy is to take the piss
Out of the opponents; the ones all love to hate
A paean to cricket – gosh, it's great.

Nightmare

Last night I woke
Without an 'I'
No thought
No word
No deed
Last night I woke
And for a second
Or an eternity
All there was
Was time.
No sense
No presence or prescience
No body.

Last night I woke
And woke again.
What will happen
If next time
I simply wake?

Not an ending

There are those things that end and then
Nothing comes of them;
And then there are those things that end
And yet there remains an essence of being
That remains alive.
Consider a School of Humanities –
A place where scholars gather
To consider the human condition.
No answers, perhaps, and yet the questions
Echo from age to age and find
A natural resonance in such a school.
Listen to rhythms of the disciplines:
Philosophy, Anthropology,
Classics and Linguistics
Sociology, History,
English and Education
Politics in its many forms;
A cauldron fired by passions unfettered
By the spreadsheet and the database
By accounts rendered and received
Brought to an exhilarating boil by ideas
And imagination,
By futures imagined from the past.
Such places as this do not end
But live beyond geography
In a world of ideas
That is peopled by such as we;
Despite those others,
Who live elsewhere.

On the feralness of nature

A while ago I discovered
that 'Nature red in tooth and claw'
is not personification
it is accurately representational
of reality

Behold my shin
the result of a sly wave
and a rock
heavily disguised by water
and waving weed

A trap devised cunningly
which, all unsuspecting
I entered and was snared
By these perfidious acolytes
Of the crimson-coated curmudgeon

Why Not to End It All

Neither beginning nor ending, Life is.
Life is
And sustains itself, non-referentially and uncritically
Life is
And all those things that attach to life
That we use to justify behaviour
Are but a vapour in the great sky of existence
Here today and tomorrow, gone
We build and make
In desperate hope of providing a meaning to life,
Calling Life our life, seeking a reason for it,
When there is no need for meaning

Life is

Time and space are intimately joined,
The warp and weft of the universal tapestry
Binding together the awful distance
Between the beauty of the stars.
The mistake, perhaps
Is thinking that because we are
The stuff of stars
That life is intimately a part of
Time and space
But not so – it springs from,
But is not of –
It comes and goes,
A vagrant breeze,
Duration, not substance.

The arid sky of time and space
Has blown away the vapour of Life
Again and again and again.
Desperate to maintain that errant steam,
We justify our place
In the Great Scheme
Erroneously assuming that there is a scheme.
Human error,
From which springs
Plane crashes and suicide bombers.

Life is.

And just as well may not be
But, it seems, needs to be,
From time to time.
So, ultimately, there is no ending

When we rage against the various
Attacks on life, personalising them
And ask why me, or her or him
Or them
Raising our fists against Fate, or God,
Or whatever evil intellect that planned
These wicked deeds, these obscenities,
We are merely whistling into a heedless void.

If there is an answer,
It is an echo only of a previous cry
Perhaps a common chord, a thread
That binds Life to life
And from which, perhaps,
A faint but warming hope emerges,
A hint of meaning that can sustain us.

Life is

And all that it entails is not to do with power
Or with greed, or courage or laziness
Or hope or charity
But all to do with need,
That heedless drive to live
That we explain and justify
Through appeals to all those things that we claim
Makes a life worth living
And like a taxidermist, we flesh out behaviour
In ourselves and other things,
Like lions and spiders and wombats
Making large claims
That are just piss and wind.

So where is meaning?
Why live, why not exist
Merely?
Meaning lies not in the intellect,
That sly deceitful demon,
But in the impulse,
The sudden urge,
In various epiphanies
From which spring
Knowledge beyond reason,
The fundamental clichés
Love and beauty
The inexpressibles
Made trite by language
And diminished by reason.
Which is one reason
Love poems
Escape me.
But in waking beside my wife
And in reading my grandson a story
And seeing my children prosper
And teaching
There is meaning.

No general rule applies
But all that is human has this meaning,
No matter how denied
And denied.

Schwenck and Furtwängler

I'd like to meet Schwenk and Furtwängler, those copious
researchers of note.
Are they Prussian, with white coats and moustaches?
Or do they just look like ordinary blokes?
Do they speak with thick German accents?
When presenting their research results?
Have they thick lenses and plastic-framed spectacles
Und sink der ozzer rezurchers ist dolts?

I don't wish to be stereotypical, maybe they're not male at all,
Perhaps they're women who've carved reputations
In the annals of academe's halls
But still, I envisage them typecast, with the lab-coats and
glasses and mo's
In a basement, somvere in Prussia,
In der Alps, mit der ice und der snow.
In der mysterious blauen-glow von compuders,
Mit der eyebrowen all bushy und grey.
Zey write mit der chalk on der blackboard
Vat zey are up to, no one can say!

Pl = J+Pa

Well done, Pa! You said
And I, ridiculously pleased
Smiled;
As if a throw and a tickle
Was equivalent to
The discovery of
The Grand Unified Theory.
I wonder if Einstein
Wanted a grandchild
More?

John

I don't care what anyone else says,
My grandson is a genius;
Maybe ingenuous
At times inept
Small.
Sure.
But then,
So was Mozart!

Don't You Just Love It?

There should be more words for love
Particularly for
The heart-bursting
Gut-wrenching
Ineffable
Joyful
Experience
When a grandson says
It's time for you to read me a story, Pa.

In life, there are few privileges:

The kiss of a child
A caress, love-kindled
A life well-lived.
A memory of one who is loved;
And one who loved in return,
Warm on a cold night.
Few privileges,
But enough
And more than enough.

Outside 1

Beach scene
Light, translucent westerly
Sand riffles under feet, bare;
Toes curling through the brightness
Sun shines
Small, foam-rimmed waves
Slap swimmers playfully
Inside
By the gym, near the pool
In the Boardroom,
Mints and water carafes –
Air conditioned cool.
Windows, curtained and tinted
Eyes on the Powerpoint
Mind on the beach
Mint in the mouth
Spirit surfing.

Acknowledgements

My particular thanks to Ricardo (Rick) Thompson, for his work on the cover design of *Veranda People*. Rick is a multitalented graphic designer, artist and excellent friend and adviser. Thanks also to my friends and colleagues of the Central Coast Poets Inc., whose advice and encouragement were a springboard into this anthology. My wife, Barbara d'Arbon, is an excellent editor and proofreader, whose gentle advice and suggestions are an integral part of this text. It's love, actually.

My daughters, Melanie and Shona, who have inherited a quirky sense of humour and a capacity for insightful (and ironic) commentary, have provided me with creative stimulation, as have their husbands. The grandchildren, a couple of whom appear in this anthology, require at least one more complete book of poems.

The title is from a poem which was highly commended in the 2004 Roland Robinson Literary Award of 2004. Other poems have appeared in a variety of anthologies, particularly from several Henry Kendall Poetry Award anthologies, organised by Central Coast Poets Inc. 'High Noon' is dedicated to my brother, Steve d'Arbon, whose lone stand against tyranny is a high point in my political development. The penknife has, for me, become a symbol of protest that has stayed with me for over sixty years.

Finally, thanks to all those others who have contributed to this anthology either as unwitting subjects or as informal editors, proofreaders and encouragers.

Mark d'Arbon, 2018

www.ingramcontent.com/pod-product-compliance
Lightning Source LLC
Chambersburg PA
CBHW070940080526
44589CB00013B/1585